HEINEMANN Profiles

Amelia Earhart

An Unauthorized Biography

Sean Connolly

Heinemann Library
Chicago, Illinois

© 2001 Reed Educational & Professional Publishing
Published by Heinemann Library, an imprint of Reed Educational & Professional Publishing,
100 N. LaSalle, Suite 1010
Chicago, IL 60602
Customer Service 888-454-2279
Visit our website at www.heinemannlibrary.com

Designed by Visual Image
Originated by Dot Gradations
Printed and bound in Hong Kong/China

05 04 03 02 01
10 9 8 7 6 5 4 3 2 1

Library of Congress Cataloging-in-Publication Data
Connolly, Sean.
    Amelia Earhart / Sean Connolly.
       p. cm. –– (Heinemann profiles)
    Includes bibliographical references and index.
    Summary: Examines the life and disappearance of the pilot who was the first woman to
cross the Atlantic in a plane by herself.
    ISBN 1-57572-223-2 (lib. bdg.)
    1. Earhart, Amelia, 1897-1937—Juvenile literature. 2. Women air pilots—United
States—Biography—Juvenile literature. [1. Earhart, Amelia, 1897-1937. 2. Air pilots. 3.
Women—Biography.] I. Title. II. Series.
TL540.E3 C66 2000
629.13'092—dc21
[B]
                                        99-089879

ELM   12944
AB 862
2000
16.95

Acknowledgments
The Publishers would like to thank the following for permission to reproduce photographs: Corbis, pp. 4, 8,
16, 23, 24, 27, 35, 37, 38, 40, 46, 51; National Aviation Museum, pp. 12, 15; Hulton-Deutsch, pp. 26, 45, 47;
Hulton Getty, pp. 29, 30, 32, 42, 44; Purdue University Libraries, pp. 6, 10, 18, 20, 28, 33, 43, 49, 50, 53; Rex
Features, p. 48.

Cover photograph reproduced with permission of E.T. Archive.

Some words are shown in bold, **like this.** You can find out what they mean by looking
in the glossary.

This is an unauthorized biography. The subject has not sponsored or endorsed this book.

CONTENTS

WHO WAS AMELIA EARHART?

A melia Earhart was one of the great American heroes of the twentieth century. She was born just a few years before the first airplane left the ground in North Carolina and although her life was short, her name has become permanently linked with flying. Like America's other flying hero of the early twentieth century, Charles Lindbergh, Amelia Earhart seemed to symbolize everything that was good about her country—its willingness to take risks, the sense of fairness and decency, and a "never give up" attitude.

MYSTERY AND TRIUMPH

Unfortunately, it is for Amelia's death—as much as for her life—that many people remember her. She and her **navigator,** Frederick Noonan, disappeared in the middle of the shark-infested Pacific in 1937 as they neared the end of a flight around the world. The disappearance has sparked many mystery theories: books have been written and special Pacific missions launched to try to find

Amelia Earhart's face was familiar to millions of people around the world.

the answer about what really happened more than sixty years ago.

What is known about Amelia Earhart, though, is the special role she played in helping the entire **aviation** industry develop. She learned to be a pilot less than twenty years after planes were invented, and went on to set—and break—many records for long-distance flights and altitude. She proudly hailed each triumph not so much as a personal success, but as proof that women could make their mark in every walk of life.

A LASTING EXAMPLE

Amelia grew up in the rural heartland of the Midwest and experienced hard times while she was young. Her successful career, however, took her into a different world of presidents and royalty, business leaders and university heads. It is to Amelia's lasting credit that she was able to remain very much the same person throughout her life—with her feet on the ground and her head in the clouds.

"I accept these rewards on behalf of the cake bakers and all of those other women who can do some things quite as important, if not more important, than flying, as well as in the name of women flying today."

Amelia Earhart,
after being voted Outstanding American Woman of 1932

CHILDHOOD

A melia Earhart was born on July 24, 1897, in the small town of Atchison, Kansas. Atchison stands on the banks of the Missouri River, and for several decades in the mid–1800s was the last **outpost** for pioneer families setting off to build new lives in the West. It is likely that in Amelia's time, there were still vivid memories of those pioneering days, and of the courageous spirit of those families.

The comfortable Earhart home reflected the family's importance in Atchison.

EARLY COMFORTS

Amelia's early life was fairly comfortable. The Earharts were somewhat important in their small town.

Millie and Pidge

Muriel, Amelia's sister, was two and a half years younger, and the two children were very close. From earliest childhood they called each other by affectionate nicknames—Amelia was "Millie" and Muriel was "Pidge." The two girls would spend hours reading together, imagining themselves to be explorers, horsewomen, or romantic heroines.

Edwin Earhart loved to spend time with his daughters, Amelia (left) and Muriel.

Amelia's father, Edwin, was a lawyer, and her mother's father, Alfred Otis, was a judge. Amelia's mother, Amy, had been a little spoiled by the judge, but she had also shown a daring streak, which Amelia **inherited**. During a trip to Colorado in 1890, Amy had become the first woman to climb Pike's Peak, a famous mountain in the Rockies.

A FATHER'S ROLE

Life in Atchison was sometimes difficult for Amelia's father. Edwin felt that Amy's father, Judge Otis, believed that he was not good enough to marry Amy. The judge's position in the community was secure and people looked up to him, but Edwin was only a young and inexperienced lawyer. In order to prove himself to the judge, Edwin hatched a number of money-making plans that never quite worked. Once he spent many hours developing a device to fasten signal flags to trains. He then traveled all the

An enormous Ferris wheel was one of the main attractions at the 1904 World's Fair in St. Louis, Missouri.

way to Washington, D.C. to **patent** it, only to find that someone else had already patented a similar invention. His trip and application fee had cost a great deal of money, and Edwin had to sell many of his possessions when he returned home.

Later, just when money matters were improving, Edwin spent more than $100—a large amount in those days—to take the family to the 1904 **World's Fair** in St. Louis. Amelia's grandparents thought this trip was a huge waste of money, but Amelia and Muriel had a wonderful time. Amelia had been particularly impressed by the roller coaster at the World's Fair. When the family returned to Kansas, she built a makeshift roller coaster out of planks in the backyard. The girls' mother thought that this was too dangerous, and ordered them to take it down.

Edwin, however, enjoyed it when the girls had tomboyish fun. Both girls were extremely fond of their father. He played with them often, usually the sorts of games boys would play. He took them fishing and even gave Amelia a small rifle to "clear the barn of rats" when she was nine years old. Amelia's grandparents did not approve of this gift, which they thought was not safe for a child of that age—especially a girl.

A NEW MOVE

Edwin Earhart continued to try to make life more comfortable for his family. Instead of coming up with daring plans, however, he concentrated on his work as a lawyer. One of his regular **clients** was a railroad company, the Rock Island Line. Edwin's work on their behalf impressed the company owners, and in 1905, they offered him a permanent job. Such a job, with its regular salary, was just what the Earharts needed, so Edwin accepted readily.

Taking the new job, however, meant that the family would have to move to the city of Des Moines, Iowa, about 150 miles (240 kilometers) to the northeast. Amelia's parents left immediately to find a new home there, leaving the girls with their grandparents for a few weeks until the new house was arranged.

"Father was loving, generous, but impractical."
Muriel Earhart, in later life

A TEST OF CHARACTER

The Earhart sisters shared many interests, like dressing up and playing with animals.

T he few weeks that the Earhart girls planned to spend with their grandparents turned out to be much longer. The girls missed their parents, who took some time finding a suitable home in Des Moines. Life in the Otis house was comfortable, though, and their grandparents loved having them. Two of their cousins lived nearby, so they always had playmates. Although the Otises would not allow the same sort of tomboyish games that Edwin Earhart encouraged, Amelia and Muriel could play in the family orchard, barn, and private park.

Amelia loved horses and became a good rider during this time. She experimented with saddles and bridles, learning just how to make them fit comfortably on the horses. She and Muriel would even ride imaginary ponies when they were inside. The Otises encouraged reading, so the girls had a good choice of books and magazines filled with adventure stories. They attended a small **private school** during their stay with the Otises, and Amelia did especially well in reading, writing, English, math, French, and sewing.

TOGETHER AGAIN

In 1908, Amelia and Muriel joined their parents in Des Moines. They loved being together again, but missed some of the advantages of living with the Otises. At their new home, there was no orchard or park, but the girls continued with their imaginary games and their reading. *Black Beauty*, a famous story about horses, was one of Amelia's favorite books.

HARD TIMES

After several happy years in Des Moines, life in the Earhart household changed for the worse. Edwin began drinking heavily and finally lost his job because he was drunk so often at work. Their comfortable way of life was gone, and the girls' mother had to work hard to

First impression

Amelia saw her first airplane in 1908 at the Iowa State Fair in Des Moines. Airplanes were still a **novelty,** but Amelia was less interested in the plane than she was in some of the other attractions— rather surprising for someone who would later become famous as a pilot!

The new invention

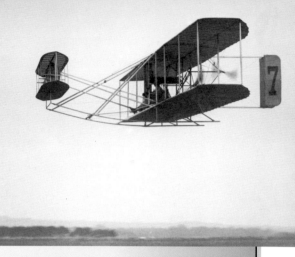

The Wright brothers, Wilbur (1867–1912) and Orville (1871–1948) invented the first successful airplane. Though they were trained as bicycle mechanics, they used their workshop in Ohio to experiment with different types of wings and propellers. Their first flight, with Orville as pilot, took place at Kitty Hawk, North Carolina, on December 17, 1903. The brothers became famous overnight and toured the country with demonstrations of their plane. For many years afterward, other pioneer pilots demonstrated their flying skills at fairs and carnivals around the United States.

make ends meet. Amelia had never needed to work before, but now her sewing skills came in handy as she used old curtains to make dresses.

In 1914, Edwin was offered another job, but found that the post was filled when he arrived for work. For Amy, this disappointment, coupled with Edwin's drinking, was the last straw. She decided to leave Edwin and take the girls to stay with some friends in Chicago. The three lived with their friends until they found a small apartment. The girls attended several different schools, and Amelia continued to study hard and get good grades. She **graduated** from Hyde Park High School in 1916.

A NEW CHANCE

Meanwhile, Edwin had been trying to overcome his drinking problem. He seemed to have succeeded, so in the summer of 1916, Amy took the girls to join him in Kansas City. Amy's mother had died, leaving her some money, so she sent the girls to **private schools** to prepare them for college. Most of the leading colleges and universities in the United States were along the East Coast, and many schools that prepared students for college were also located there. Amelia attended the Ogontz School in Pennsylvania, which was near the college of her choice, Bryn Mawr. Muriel went to a school in Toronto, Canada.

After a Christmas visit with Muriel in early 1918, Amelia decided to leave school and move to Toronto. Canada was involved in **World War I,** and Amelia joined the war effort working as a volunteer nurse at the Spadina Military Hospital. In the last year of the war, there was a terrible **epidemic** of a serious type of influenza, and thousands of people—including many wounded soldiers—became sick. Amelia, weakened by long hours of hard work, also came down with this illness. She had to stay in bed for several weeks, and she was still recovering when the war ended on November 11, 1918. The time that Amelia spent in Toronto showed her courage and willingness to make sacrifices. It also introduced her to what was to become her main passion—flying.

The "Flying Bug"

I n the early winter of 1918, Amelia went to an airfield near Toronto to visit some of the men she had treated at the hospital. While she was there, she watched the pilots practicing takeoffs, landings, and other **maneuvers** in small **biplanes**. Unlike her first experience with airplanes ten years before, when she had not been very impressed, this time she was fascinated.

Many airmen, like the pilots that Amelia watched, had learned how to fly during **World War I**. The United States had entered the war in the last year, and many Americans served as wartime pilots. After the war, these same pilots were trying to find ways of using their flying skills in peacetime. Many of them chose to earn their living by **barnstorming**— touring around the United States and Canada and showing off their flying ability.

Serious issues

There were other concerns for Amelia at this time. One of them was the struggle for women's right to vote. With her own tomboyish upbringing, Amelia had always felt that girls and women should have

"I remember the sting of the snow on my face when it was blown back from the propellers when the training plane took off on skis."

Amelia Earhart, *The Fun of It*

Early biplanes looked flimsy as they edged shakily into the air.

the same chance as boys and men to learn, work, and vote for their leaders. She strongly supported the **women's suffrage** movement, and expressed her views clearly in her letters to Muriel and her mother. Women finally gained the right to vote in the United States two years later, in 1920, and Amelia welcomed the change. She had always had a strong belief in women's **capabilities,** and several years later, her groundbreaking achievements made Amelia Earhart a household name around the world. Amelia's views were ahead of her time in this respect, since at that time many people—including many women themselves—believed that only men should have the right to vote or to hold important jobs.

Amelia Earhart's official Columbia University photograph shows a bit of mischief twinkling in her eyes.

I n keeping with her views on women's **potential,** Amelia enrolled in an all-female class on how to repair car engines. Her studious nature and natural curiosity helped her learn about the inner workings of an engine. This knowledge helped her later when she became a pilot.

GOING WEST

Amelia and Muriel both started college during the fall of 1919. Muriel went to Smith College in Massachusetts, and Amelia began studying medicine at Columbia University in New York. Although she concentrated hard on her work, she also had a lot of fun. Once, she climbed to the top of the dome of the university library and was photographed there wearing a big straw hat. By the spring of 1920, however, Amelia was receiving letters from both parents asking her to join them in California. Edwin had found a new job there, but Amy wanted Amelia's support because their relationship was still somewhat tense. Amelia had to leave college and travel across the country to the West Coast.

The Earharts' house was large, and they rented out rooms to earn more money. A young man named Sam Chapman rented one of the rooms. He came from the East Coast, so Amelia felt comfortable exploring her new surroundings with him. Their friendship deepened, and the two became engaged. In reality, though, Amelia and Sam did not make a very good match. He wanted a traditional wife who would stay at home, and Amelia's independent spirit would never have allowed that.

ATTRACTED AGAIN

It was not long after Amelia's arrival in California that she found herself among airplanes again. Her father took her to an air display near Los Angeles and paid for Amelia to have a ten-minute flight. Amelia was thrilled and excited to be in the air, and she decided to learn how to be a pilot herself. She announced this news to her family that evening. Neither parent seemed to object, so Amelia started looking for ways to make her dream come true.

"I'll see what I can do to keep Mother and Dad together, Pidge, but after that I'm going to come back here and live my own life."
Amelia Earhart, writing to her sister before going to California

"As soon as we left the ground I knew myself I had to fly."
Amelia Earhart, *The Fun of It*

LESSONS IN THE SKY

A melia's first flight took place at Rogers Field, situated along Wilshire Boulevard, one of the busiest roads in Los Angeles. It is hard to imagine an airfield so close to the heart of a great city today, but when Amelia took her first flight, airplanes were still very new. They had been around for less than twenty years, and the sound of whirring propellers or the sight of a **biplane** edging its way skyward would draw dozens of interested spectators. Most were interested by the whole idea of flying, but few were daring enough to get on board an airplane, and fewer still would consider being pilots themselves. Amelia Earhart was one of those few— and one of the only women brave enough to join that very small circle of daring **aviators.**

Amelia and Frank Hawks met again some years after he took her on her first flight in 1920.

A DARING INSTRUCTOR

Amelia's father had agreed to her learning to fly, but he felt he couldn't afford the total cost of lessons, which was about $1,000—a great deal of money. Amelia was **persistent,** though, and eventually Edwin decided to pay for the first few lessons. He also made one condition: the instructor had to be a woman, because he did not want Amelia to be alone with a man in an airplane. Amelia agreed, because she felt that she could learn better from a woman. She soon found out about a woman pilot nearby who also gave flying lessons.

The pilot's name was Anita Snook, although her friends called her "Neta." She was, if anything, even more determined to prove women's **potential** than Amelia was herself.

Neta Snook

Neta had learned to fly just before the United States entered **World War I,** and had even tried to become a fighter pilot in the American armed forces. The U.S. government would not allow women to fly, so Neta spent the war helping the British Royal Air Force take care of their aircraft. Like the pilots whom Amelia had met in Toronto, Neta was determined to continue flying after the war. She bought a beat-up Canadian plane, called a Canuck, and restored it herself. Neta took her plane across the United States, earning money by **barnstorming**, before setting up a flying company in Los Angeles.

AERIAL FRIENDSHIP

Neta agreed to be Amelia's flying teacher. So, on January 3, 1921, Amelia arrived at the airfield dressed as she felt a pilot should be—in a full set of riding clothes. She found out, however, that for the first few weeks lessons were based on the ground. She learned the basics of how planes fly, how the engines work, and how to predict the weather.

It was at this stage that Amelia and Sam Chapman started to have doubts about getting married. Amelia was taking risks that Sam felt were not appropriate for women. Also, Amelia worked at two jobs—in a telephone office and in her father's business—to earn money for lessons. She spent her free time in Neta's **hangar,** getting to know more about planes and flying. She was too busy to spend time with Sam.

Neta Snook (left) was a good pilot, and she became one of Amelia's closest friends.

ON HER OWN

Amelia particularly loved her lessons in the air and spent about six months learning from Neta in the two-seater Canuck. Then she became interested in buying a plane of her own. She used her earnings and borrowed some money from her family to buy a new plane from Bert Kinner, an **aviation engineer** who built planes in Los Angeles. She called the yellow plane "the Canary."

An expensive hobby?

Amelia's first plane cost $2,000. To pay for it, she took on jobs as a photographer and even as a driver of a truck hauling gravel.

Amelia still needed a copilot, so Neta continued their lessons in the new Kinner Airster. One day, Amelia and Neta were flying around Los Angeles when the plane wouldn't climb fast enough to clear a stand of trees. Amelia, at the controls, had to pull the plane up quickly, making it **stall**. The plane plummeted to the ground nose-first. Neither woman was hurt, and the plane was only slightly damaged, but it was Amelia's first crash.

This experience did not scare Amelia away from flying, though. In fact, not long afterward, she made her first solo flight in the Canary and celebrated the occasion by buying herself a new leather flying coat. Now she felt that she was a real pilot.

FLYING TO FAME

A melia dedicated herself to flying, using every opportunity to take her Kinner plane on trips around southern California. Flying was an expensive business, and most pilots struggled to find enough money to pay for fuel. Amelia was no exception, and her earnings that had been used for lessons now paid for fuel for her airplane.

A RARE BREED

Amelia's friend Neta left Los Angeles at the end of 1921, leaving Amelia as the only woman pilot at her familiar airfield. She got along well with the men who worked around the airfield, and she put her knowledge of car mechanics to use while learning more about how airplane engines operated. In the small world of flying in the early 1920s, Amelia became a local celebrity. The *Los Angeles Examiner* newspaper printed a long interview with her in 1922.

"The only time a lady's name should appear in print is at her birth, her marriage, and her funeral."

Amelia Earhart's uncle, after seeing her featured in the *New York Times*

By October 1922, Amelia was confident enough to try for a flying record. Without telling them why she wanted them there, she invited her family members to a local airfield. Her reason became clear when she joined them in the stands later. Amelia had taken her plane up and established a women's altitude record of 14,000 feet (4,267 meters).

It was not all glory for Amelia, however. She had her share of crash-landings, with bumps and bruises to show for them. Still, these sorts of adventures made Amelia even more famous, and her reputation spread throughout the United States. Her altitude record and her daring flying made her name familiar to many newspaper readers. In October 1923, shortly after she earned her official pilot's license, she was featured in a lengthy article in the *New York Times*.

Amelia's altitude record was soon broken by Ruth Nichols (center), her friend and rival.

CONCERNS ON THE GROUND

Amelia respected and cared for her mother, Amy.

The following year, 1924, began with tension and unhappiness for Amelia Earhart. Her parents were not getting along, and in the spring, they agreed to a divorce. Amy was upset by these events, and Amelia felt a need to help her mother. They decided to travel across the country to join Muriel, who was working in Boston. Amelia sold her plane—a more advanced Kinner—and bought a car. Then the pair took a deliberately roundabout route to reach Boston. Amelia knew that her mother would benefit from this adventure, so she made sure that they took in as much scenery and excitement as they could. By the time they arrived, they had driven 7,000 miles (11,265 kilometers).

A social conscience

Amelia found herself in Boston with no plane and no **income**. As someone who loved to stay active, this meant that she had to find something to keep herself busy. Amelia answered an advertisement and became a **social worker** in a house for **immigrants** who spoke little English. She set to work with her usual enthusiasm and energy, helping the mainly Syrian and Chinese immigrants become acquainted with their new country. Amelia went far beyond her official job of teaching them English and helping the adults find jobs. She organized outings and drove her new friends around in her beat-up car, which she called "the Yellow Peril."

A BUSINESS PROSPECT

With a regular salary coming in, Amelia was also able to think about flying again. Bert Kinner contacted a Boston businessman, who asked Amelia to join a project to develop a new airport near Boston. Amelia put some of her own money into the project, thereby becoming a company **director.** Even more importantly, her connection with the airport gave Amelia the chance to fly again.

By 1926, Amelia was in the air whenever she got the chance, flying to festivals in the Boston area and helping to **promote** not just the new airfield, but flying in general. Her well-groomed appearance and sincere talk about the pleasures of flying made her a walking advertisement for flying itself.

A FATEFUL PHONE CALL

Charles Lindbergh's solo flight across the Atlantic in May 1927 kept the topic of flying in the headlines for months. Lindbergh had not been the first person to cross the Atlantic; other **crews** had crossed it before. Lindbergh's flight stood out because it was a solo effort. What other challenges could exist in flying across the Atlantic Ocean?

THE FIRST WOMAN

The answer was becoming clear among those who flew: all that was left was for a woman to fly across the Atlantic. By 1928, several female **aviators** began planning to do just that. One of them was Mrs. Amy Guest, a rich American who lived in London. Her own family felt that the flight was too risky for Amy

Hilton Railey suggested that Amelia Earhart try to become the first woman to fly across the Atlantic.

herself, and convinced her to find a replacement pilot. Mrs. Guest wanted to choose a well–spoken woman who would fit into English society. Hilton Railey, a friend of Mrs. Guest, learned of just such a pilot. In late April 1928, he put a call through to Boston and asked to speak to Miss Amelia Earhart.

The *Spirit of St. Louis*

In May 1927, an event occurred that took the world by storm. Until that time, all long-distance solo flights had been done over land, so that pilots could make emergency landings if the weather turned bad or the plane ran into trouble. Then, on May 20, 1927, 25-year-old Charles Lindbergh set off from an airfield near New York in the plane he called the *Spirit of St. Louis*: He landed in Paris 33 hours, 30 minutes later. The whole world hailed Lindbergh as a hero. Even after the celebrations ended on both sides of the Atlantic, Lindbergh's achievement remained a shining example of heroism and daring. The world wanted to know all about "Lucky Lindy," and publishers competed to tell his story. Such a book would sell many copies, making both Lindbergh and the publisher very rich. The man who won the **publishing rights** to tell Lindbergh's story was George Putnam, who would soon become important in Amelia Earhart's life.

The *Friendship* Flight

Hilton Railey asked Earhart to meet him in his Boston office to discuss a dangerous and exciting flying mission. By early May, Earhart had learned of the real nature of the trip and had accepted. Mrs. Guest and the other organizers were pleased with their choice, since Earhart struck them as being capable, well-spoken, and daring.

Careful planning

Amelia Earhart was the only woman in a three-person **crew** that included two other experienced **aviators**—Wilmer Stultz and Louis Gordon. They decided to take off from Canada in a three-engine **amphibious** plane called the *Friendship*. The flight from Trepassey, Newfoundland, to Europe would take place in May, exactly a year after Lindbergh's trip. It was kept secret—Amelia did not even tell her family.

Bad weather delayed the mission, and the *Friendship* finally left Boston for Newfoundland on June 3. Two weeks later, it was ready to go, but the plane could not take off under the weight of all its fuel. The crew dumped some of the fuel, leaving what they hoped was just enough, and finally took off at around noon on June 17, 1928.

Earhart Plane Soaring
Over the Atlantic;
Reported Nearly
Halfway to Ireland
Eight Hours After
Leaving Trepassey
New York Times
headline, June 18,
1928

ACROSS THE SEA

The news of the flight had become public in early June. Once the *Friendship* took off, the world watched and waited. The crew took the plane up above the clouds. Amelia checked the maps and wrote in the flight log book as the plane flew through the night.

After her flight, Amelia Earhart described it to eager reporters.

The next morning, the crew looked down and saw several ships. They discussed whether it would be safer to stop there or to watch for dry land. They chose to continue, and finally saw land about an hour and a half later. They managed to land on a stretch of water near a small town. It was hard to believe that they were now on the other side of the Atlantic, less than 24 hours after taking off in Newfoundland.

TOAST OF THE WORLD

T he **crew** of the *Friendship* had certainly crossed the Atlantic, but they had missed their expected target—Ireland—by several hundred miles. Instead, they had traveled farther, and landed at Burry Port, in southern Wales.

SLOW BUILD-UP

Unlike Lindbergh's arrival in Paris in 1927, when dozens of French cars illuminated the darkened runway with their headlights and the crowd's roar drowned out the engine noise, the *Friendship*'s arrival was low-key. Several railway workers walked

While in England, Earhart enjoyed a trip in a Moth plane.

to the waterfront, looked the plane over, and returned to their work. It was nearly an hour before the first boats came out to greet the fliers and take them ashore.

The crew contacted Hilton Railey, who had sailed across the Atlantic before them and was waiting in Southampton, England. He arrived a few hours later with a journalist from the *New York Times*. By now, the residents of Burry Port realized that they were witnessing history, and thousands of onlookers crowded around the plane and its crew.

After spending the night in Wales, the crew woke the next morning to find a sackful of **telegrams** congratulating them. One of them, from U.S. President Calvin Coolidge, read, "to you the first woman successfully to **span** the North Atlantic by air the great admiration of myself and the United States."

Singled out

It is interesting to note that the president's telegram was addressed to Earhart and made no mention of the other two crew members. Earhart was distressed by this **omission** and the many others like it that followed. It became clear that the public was fascinated by her achievement as the first woman to fly across the Atlantic, and that Stultz and Gordon were considered to have just "gone along for the ride."

ONE BIG PARTY

Amelia Earhart became an instant international celebrity. From Wales, the crew went to an even bigger reception in Southampton, and then on to London. Amy Guest insisted that Earhart stay at her Park Lane house to recover from the trip, but there was also a dizzying array of tea dances, dinner parties, Wimbledon tennis matches, and other public functions to attend. In the midst of all the parties and interviews, however, Earhart found time to visit houses where British **social workers** carried out work similar to her own in Boston.

The **crew** of the *Friendship* finally sailed back to the United States. The reception there was even bigger, with huge parades in New York, Boston, and Chicago.

THE BENEFITS OF FAME

Earhart, who was called "Lady Lindy" after Charles Lindbergh, was in much demand after her return

Huge crowds lined the Southampton docks to welcome the *Friendship*.

Earhart (far left) met with Charles Lindbergh (far right) and others in 1929.

home. She gave lectures, helped **edit** magazines, and wrote a book about her adventure, entitled *20 Hrs. 40 Min*. Overseeing many of these commitments was publisher George Putnam, who had helped organize and publicize the *Friendship* journey.

Earhart's reputation was good for the **aviation** industry, and in July 1929, she won the job of assistant to the general traffic manager of Transcontinental Air Transport. But Earhart continued to fly, and in August 1929, she placed third in an all-women's air race, the Women's Air Derby from Santa Monica to Cleveland. In the same year, she helped organize the Ninety-Nines, a supportive group for women in aviation. She seemed to have the best of all possible worlds.

"It was then that we came to realize how much water we had passed over in the *Friendship*. Eastbound, the mileage had been measured in clouds, not water. There had never been adequate comprehension of the Atlantic below."

Amelia Earhart, describing her crossing back to America by ship

A PARTNER FOR LIFE

O ne thing that Earhart did not have during her period of international fame in the late 1920s was a husband. Amelia Earhart was not the sort of woman who needed a man to do things for her, but she had always had a romantic nature, and enjoyed the idea of having someone with whom she could share her life. She was over thirty; in those days, most women her age were already married, and many of the rest were actively seeking to be married. Seeing the troubles in her own parents' marriage had made her cautious, however. It also probably explains why she didn't rush to marry Sam Chapman when they were engaged in California.

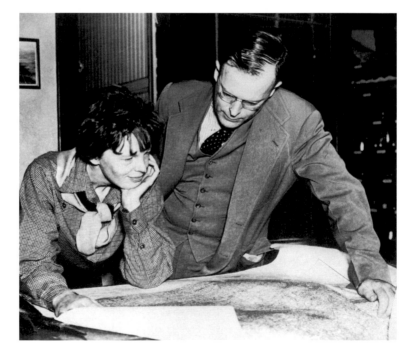

George Putnam and Amelia Earhart worked together on some of her flight plans.

EQUAL FOOTING

Earhart's relationship with George Putnam was very different. From the start, he recognized her adventurous spirit and even encouraged it. True, George was a successful publisher and businessman, but he also enjoyed rolling up his sleeves and going on long trips. Amelia found these qualities very attractive, and their relationship deepened. George, however, was already married—although the marriage was not a happy one.

George and his wife, Dorothy Binney, were divorced in December 1929. Reporters soon began asking George and Amelia when they would marry. The couple kept very quiet about the matter. Then, on February 7, 1931, they got married in George's mother's house in Connecticut. There were no guests, and the only witnesses were George's mother, an uncle, the local judge, and the judge's son.

GOING SOLO

At the time of her wedding to George Putnam in early 1931, Amelia Earhart seemed to have everything she could possibly want. She was married to a man she loved and respected. She was famous around the world, and could count Charles Lindbergh, Winston Churchill, and many business leaders among her **acquaintances.** Just as important, during the terrible economic time known as the **Great Depression,** she had a large and secure fortune from all her writings, lectures, and business involvements. The only thing that was lacking was the very thing that always drove her on in life—a good challenge.

THE ATLANTIC AGAIN

The challenge that Earhart chose was another crossing of the Atlantic, although this time she planned to make the flight solo. The main idea behind this was a personal challenge—a chance to prove to herself that she could do it—but there were also other reasons. After Earhart's triumph in 1928, some critics claimed that her involvement with that flight had been exaggerated and that she had merely been a passenger.

George Putnam, who took a hand in planning Earhart's career, learned that some other women

aviators had the same idea of crossing the Atlantic alone. If any of them succeeded, then Amelia might not be the world's most famous female pilot any more. She would have fewer opportunities to earn money through her fame.

SECRET PLANS

By early 1932, Amelia and George had agreed on a plan. Earhart owned a Lockheed Vega, a plane that had proved its quality and **durability** in flights up and down the East Coast. However, for a transatlantic flight it needed to be **modified** to take a larger engine and fuel tanks. If other people saw Earhart's plane being changed in this way, they would know her plan. So Earhart asked her friend Bernt Balchen to "borrow" the plane. Since Balchen was planning an Antarctic flight of his own, the public assumed that the work on the plane was for his journey.

Earhart examines her Lockheed Vega to see if it could face the transatlantic challenge.

THE ADVENTURE BEGINS

George had worked out the date of the flight well in advance. It would be May 20, 1932, exactly five years after Lindbergh's heroic flight. Earhart would take off from Newfoundland again, and Balchen had the plane ready by mid-May. Everything was in place for the flight, and the Atlantic weather forecasts, although not ideal, suggested that they could go ahead as planned.

Earhart had one last check of the plane on the morning of the flight, and then she took a nap for several hours in the afternoon. She woke, walked calmly to the plane, started it, and took off at about 7:00 in the evening. Later, she would remember seeing a perfect sunset as she began her flight over the Atlantic.

AN IRISH WELCOME

Earhart piloted the plane skillfully throughout the flight, although she had some close calls. One of these was when she took the plane up above some thick clouds. As she neared the top of the cloud bank, the plane began to feel sluggish and heavy. Earhart realized that it was covered in ice. The plane began to spin, but she brought it down to a lower altitude, where the warmer air would melt the

AE TOOK OFF 712
NFLD PERFECT
PERFORMANCE
Telegram sent to George Putnam after Amelia's takeoff

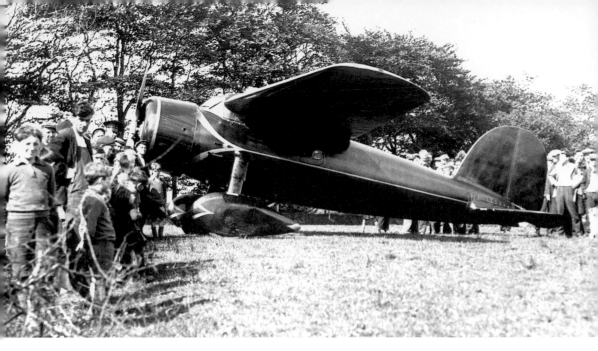

ice. She had to fly so low that she could see the
waves in the ocean. She also battled fog, a leaky fuel
tank, and engine trouble on her flight.

By daylight, Earhart was relieved to see a fishing
vessel below her. Land could not be far off.
Eventually, to her relief, she sighted the rolling,
green Irish landscape. She knew that she could not
expect to find an airfield, so she circled until she
found a suitable pasture for her landing. At exactly
1:45 P.M. on May 21, 1932, she touched down near
the village of Culmore in Northern Ireland.

A farm worker, who saw Earhart land, took her
across some fields to the nearest farmhouse. There
the owners, the Gallagher family, did what any Irish
family would do for a surprise visitor—they made
her a pot of tea.

*The people of
Culmore, Northern
Ireland, were not
used to American
pilots landing in
their fields.*

FRIENDS IN HIGH PLACES

Earhart flew a night tour of Washington, D.C. with her friend Eleanor Roosevelt, the wife of U.S. President Franklin Roosevelt.

Earhart's reception in Europe this time was even bigger than after her triumph four years earlier. Now "Lady Lindy" was truly Lindbergh's equal. Reporters flocked to Ireland to interview her, and many offered to fly her to London. Instead, Earhart flew there herself, using a plane rented by the film company that had bought movie rights to her story.

NATIONAL PRIDE

On the flight, Earhart read some congratulatory **telegrams,** from the president of the United States, the British prime minister, and Charles Lindbergh, among others. In London, there was again a whirl of social engagements.

Back in the United States, Earhart was cheered not just by the press and the public, but by important organizations. She became the first female **Honorary** Member of the National **Aeronautic** Association. At the White House, President Hoover awarded her a special gold medal made by the National Geographic Society. Again, she was the first woman to be so honored. The U.S. Congress awarded her the Distinguished Flying Cross, and the French government made her a member of the Legion of Honor.

> "AE does seem to me a particularly good sport who gets all the fun there is out of what goes on, whether it be flying or gardening or fan mail."
> George Putnam, answering criticisms that women should stay at home

LIFE AT THE TOP

Later in 1932, Franklin Roosevelt was elected president. Roosevelt was a friend of George Putnam's, so there were more trips to the White House, although these visits were informal. George also had contacts in the film industry, and Amelia got to know many Hollywood stars.

The never-ending string of social and business engagements gained Earhart money and respect, but she had no time to herself for months on end. Her only regret was that she had so little time for her main interest in life—flying.

MORE ACHIEVEMENTS

Few people were surprised when Amelia Earhart was voted Outstanding American Woman of the Year in October 1932. She used her reputation to stress the importance of women's equality and of the need to develop the **aviation** industry.

REWRITING THE RECORD BOOKS

With the 1932 flight, in addition to being the first woman to fly the Atlantic on her own, Earhart had set a number of records. Her flight of 2,026 miles (3,260 kilometers) was the longest nonstop flight by a woman, her trip had been the fastest transatlantic flight, and she had become the first person to fly across the Atlantic twice. In 1933, Earhart took two hours off her own cross-country (Los Angeles to New York) women's record, making the crossing in just over 17 hours. She then turned her attention to the Pacific Ocean.

In late 1934, Earhart decided to fly from Hawaii to California, a 2,500-mile (4,023-kilometer) flight across the Pacific. The trip had been made once before, but not by a solo flier. Several pilots had already died trying to make

Earhart was greeted by crowds wherever she went, this time on a visit to Brussels.

Huge crowds surrounded the plane after Earhart's 1935 flight from Hawaii to California.

the flight. Earhart did not seem very worried, and plans went well for the flight on January 11, 1935. As usual, able mechanics got the Lockheed ready, and George mounted a successful publicity campaign. Earhart took off in the late afternoon. The flight went exactly as planned, and Earhart touched down near San Francisco just eighteen hours after leaving Honolulu. Cheering crowds welcomed her yet again.

FRIENDLY NEIGHBORS

Earhart accepted a Mexican invitation to make a "friendship flight" from Los Angeles to Mexico City and then to New York. The flight began on April 19, 1935, and ended nearly three weeks later. She had to wait in Mexico until Mexican soldiers could build a special runway for her plane to take off. The landing at Newark Airport, near New York, was proof that Earhart was still a national hero—thousands of people crowded the runway just to glimpse the daring pilot.

"It's the first time I've ever been *asked* anywhere. I just *went* to Ireland."
Amelia Earhart, referring to her Mexican trip

THE LAST CHALLENGE

I n 1935, Amelia Earhart accepted an invitation to become part of the **faculty** at Purdue University in Indiana. She would be involved in a special department that studied careers for women. In addition, since Purdue had its own airfield and a department of **aeronautics**, Earhart could combine two of the causes that meant so much to her—inspiring women to fulfill their ambitions and promoting the cause of flying.

LAYING PLANS

The link with Purdue also gave Earhart the chance to buy an advanced airplane. The plane, a Lockheed Electra 10E, would be used as a "flying laboratory" during her future flights, so that her experiences could help teach about **aviation.** The new plane was equipped with the latest radio and **navigational** equipment, including tanks that could hold enough fuel to travel more than 4,000 miles (6,437

Earhart taught students using Purdue's "flying laboratory."

A risky proposal

The route that Earhart was planning to take was east to west, roughly along the equator. But even with the Lockheed's large fuel tanks, it would be almost impossible to travel the longest leg of the trip, across the Pacific Ocean from Hawaii to Japan. Earhart wrote to President Franklin Roosevelt, asking for U.S. Navy planes to refuel her plane in midair over the Pacific. The president agreed, but government officials later came up with a different solution. Amelia could use the new landing strip on tiny Howland Island— a piece of land less than two miles (3.2 kilometers) long and only half a mile (0.8 kilometer) wide. It would be extremely difficult to find such a small island in the middle of the world's largest ocean, but Amelia accepted the challenge.

kilometers). With such fuel **capacity** on her plane, Earhart began seriously to consider trying a flight around the world.

On February 12, 1937, Amelia and George organized a **press conference** to announce the trip. Later, she invited Frederick Noonan, an experienced **navigator,** to join her. It would be his job to figure out what direction the plane was flying, so they could find the right places to land. Also on board for part of the trip would be technical adviser Paul Mantz and radio operator Harry Manning.

Frederick Noonan helped keep the plane on course during the long journey.

The crash landing in Hawaii was a serious setback to Earhart's flight plans.

SECOND TIME LUCKY?

On March 17, 1937, the **crew** took off from Oakland Airport in California on the first leg of the trip to Hawaii. They broke the speed record by reaching Honolulu in less than sixteen hours, but had to wait 24 hours before continuing because of bad weather.

Then, at sunrise on March 20, they had a crisis. Just as the plane was building up speed to take off, it began to swerve and then turned almost completely around. The landing gear was crushed, and rescuers rushed to save the crew in case of fire. Some pilots blamed Earhart for not steering properly.

After two months, the plane was ready for a second attempt, this time heading east. On May 21, Earhart left Oakland with Frederick Noonan. George Putnam and the Lockheed mechanic, Bo McKneely, went along as far as Miami. Then, on June 1, Earhart and Noonan set off for Puerto Rico and South America. They crossed the Atlantic, made stops in Africa, and passed over Arabia before landing in Calcutta, India, on June 17. Then they continued through Thailand, Singapore, Indonesia, and Australia. On June 29, they arrived at Lae, New Guinea.

RADIO SILENCE

On July 2, Earhart and Noonan set off from Lae for the most difficult leg of the journey—to the airfield on tiny Howland Island. For six or seven hours, there were regular radio reports with Lae; then Earhart kept in contact with American ships in the area. Eighteen hours into the flight, she reported that they were "a hundred miles out" from Howland. The airfield prepared for her arrival, but in her next message, Earhart reported that they were running low on fuel and couldn't see the island. At 20:14 hours **Greenwich Mean Time (GMT),** the USS *Itasca* received its last message from Earhart's plane. And then there was silence.

Earhart's plane passed over one of America's most famous landmarks, the Golden Gate Bridge, shortly after takeoff on her first attempt to fly around the world.

"KHAQQ to *Itasca*. We are on the line of position one five seven dash three three seven. Will repeat this message on 6210 kilocycles. We are running north to south."

Amelia Earhart's last radio message, using her code letters KHAQQ

A Lingering Legacy

It was impossible to believe that America's most beloved pilot could be missing, and yet that was the truth that faced George Putnam as he paced up and down in the U.S. Coast Guard headquarters in San Francisco. He was joined by Frederick Noonan's wife, Bea, and the pair anxiously awaited any sort of news from the Pacific. It was a helpless period for George, who was used to being in control. He could do nothing except insist that the U.S. Navy make every effort to find the lost plane.

The navy, meanwhile, had sent several ships, including an aircraft carrier, to search the area around Howland Island. Over the next several days, American naval ships, particularly the battleship *Colorado*, explored the region thoroughly. Three **reconnaissance** planes from the *Colorado* searched from the air, trying to scan every island and **reef** where Earhart and Noonan might have found shelter. Only one island in the search area was **inhabited**, but the people who lived there had not heard of Earhart or seen anything unusual. The search area was expanded when no sign of the plane was found.

Howland Island was a tiny target to reach amid the vastness of the Pacific Ocean.

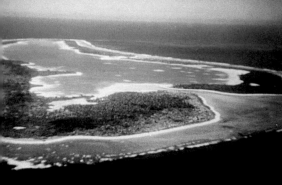

For many people, Amelia Earhart's legacy lies in her clear accounts of her daring flights.

British and Japanese ships joined the search, and it was estimated that more than 4,000 seamen from different nations were involved. More than a quarter of a million square miles (647,500 square kilometers) had been searched before the search was officially abandoned on July 18. George had to accept that his wife had died.

THE EARHART MYSTERY

The public loves a mystery, and the disappearance of Amelia Earhart remains one of the most intriguing of the twentieth century. Most people accept that the plane was probably blown off course on its way to tiny Howland Island, and that it crashed and sank in the open water. Earhart and Noonan would probably not have survived long in the water.

Last letters

In the days and weeks after Amelia's disappearance, George had an unexpectedly sad task, as many letters from his wife arrived. They had been written as part of a diary and sent from different airfields during her journey. It was difficult for George to receive and read these letters, but being a professional publisher, he collected them and had them printed as a book entitled *Last Flight*.

Others have come up with different theories about Earhart's flight and her disappearance. The Pacific was the scene of fierce fighting in **World War II,** and some people believe that Earhart was spying for the United States in the years before the war. They believe that she was captured in Japanese territory and taken prisoner. In 1944, U.S.

Earhart, shown here with movie stars Cary Grant and Myrna Loy, was a huge star in her own time.

Marines landing on the Pacific island of Saipan claimed to have found a photo album of Earhart. George Putnam made a special trip there, but he found no trace of his wife, and none of the islanders knew about her.

TYING UP LOOSE ENDS

More recently, there have been efforts to solve the mystery of Earhart's disappearance and to finish the work she started. The Earhart Project, begun in 1988, sent teams out to the Pacific to use scientific methods to discover the answer. They believe that Amelia Earhart and Frederick Noonan crashed at the **uninhabited** Nikumaroro island group. Future missions aim to provide definite evidence.

In 1997, the American pilot Linda Finch re-created Earhart's last flight in a Lockheed Electra like the one in which Amelia Earhart and Frederick Noonan had flown. Her successful flight was entitled World Flight 1997. Earhart would have celebrated her hundredth birthday in that year.

More important than the wealth of theories about Amelia Earhart's disappearance is the **legacy** that she has left. It is true that her last trip was never completed, but in some ways it is also appropriate. Through her example, she had opened the door for other women. It would be wrong to say that Amelia Earhart single-handedly caused the social advances that led to greater equality between men and women, but her life was an example of high achievement when there were many obstacles to overcome.

Amy Johnson was another female aviator whose life ended in tragedy. She drowned when her plane crashed into the Thames River in 1941.

"I want to do it because I want to do it. Women must try to do things as men have tried. When they fail their failure must be but a challenge to others."
Amelia Earhart, writing to George Putnam

AMELIA EARHART—
TIMELINE

1897	Born in Atchison, Kansas (July 24)
1904	Visits **World's Fair** in St. Louis, Missouri
1905	Stays with sister Muriel at grandparents' home while parents find new home in Iowa
1914	Moves to Chicago with mother and sister
1916	**Graduates** from Hyde Park High School, Chicago
1918	Becomes volunteer nurse in Toronto, Canada
1919	Enrolls at Columbia University, New York
1920	Leaves college to join parents in California
1921	Has first flying lessons near Los Angeles
1922	Sets women's altitude record
1923	Earns pilot's license; featured in the *New York Times*
1925	Finds a job as a **social worker** in Boston
1928	Becomes first woman to fly across the Atlantic Ocean; writes the book *20 Hrs. 40 Min.*
1929	Becomes assistant to the general traffic manager of Transcontinental Air Transport; places third in Santa Monica to Cleveland Women's Air Derby
1930	Sets women's speed record of 181.18 miles per hour; serves as vice president for public relations of New York, Philadelphia, and Washington Airways
1931	Marries publisher George Putnam
1932	Becomes first woman to fly solo across the Atlantic; voted Outstanding American Woman of the Year
1935	Completes first solo flight over Pacific from Hawaii to California; makes solo flight from Los Angeles to Mexico City; accepts post as visiting **faculty** member at Purdue University
1937	Disappears over the Pacific near the end of an around-the-world flight with **navigator** Frederick Noonan

GLOSSARY

acquaintance person someone knows, but not as a close friend

aeronautics the science of flight

amphibious for an aircraft, able to land on land and water

aviation flying in an aircraft

aviation engineer someone who studies the machinery used in powered aircraft

aviator pilot of an aircraft

barnstorming displaying flying skills to a paying audience

biplane aircraft with two pairs of wings, one above the other

capability overall ability of a person to do something

capacity in an aircraft, the amount of fuel a plane can hold

client someone who pays for the services of another person such as a lawyer

crew pilot, mechanic, and other members of a team who fly together

director someone with the power to make decisions for a company

durability ability to stand up to a great deal of wear and tear

edit to prepare a piece of writing so that it can be published

epidemic widespread outbreak of a serious disease

faculty teachers and instructors at a college or university

graduate to complete one's schooling and receive a certificate, or someone who has done so

Great Depression period (1929–39) of great poverty and hardship around the world

Greenwich Mean Time (GMT) time at the Prime Meridian. It is the international standard time.

hangar large building in which aircraft are stored

honorary awarded to show respect or recognize achievement

immigrant someone who moves permanently to a country to start a new life there

income regular supply of money earned that can be used to pay for living expenses

inhabited having people living there

inherit to be born with a trait that comes from a parent or relative, or to get money or property when a relative or friend dies

legacy what is remembered about someone after he or she dies

maneuver special drill or practice motion by a ship or plane to test the skill of the pilot or the performance of the vehicle

modified improved by adding or replacing certain parts

navigational having to do with steering or planning a course of a vehicle

navigator person who decides the course a vehicle will take

novelty something that is new and unusual

omission something that is left out, often by mistake

outpost location that is very remote

patent legal right to produce something, which also denies others the same right

persistent very determined; making many efforts to achieve something

potential possible ability of a person to do something

press conference public meeting where people answer questions from reporters

private school school at which parents, rather than local authorities, pay for the education of children

promote to talk about something publicly in order to make it more well known

publishing right legal right to print something, which others may not print

reconnaissance finding information by traveling around and reporting

reef rocky structure near the surface of the ocean, sometimes jutting out to form a small island

social worker someone who helps poor or needy people

span to stretch from one side to the other

stall for an aircraft, to lose the air speed necessary to move forward, so that it seems to briefly hang motionless in the air

telegram typewritten message sent by wire, usually in as few words as possible

uninhabited having no one living there

women's suffrage idea that women should have the same right to vote as men

World's Fair large fair that includes displays featuring the accomplishments of individual countries or international companies

World War I (1914–18) war between Germany, Austria, and their supporters against Britain, France, the United States, and their supporters

World War II (1939–45) war between Germany, Japan, and their supporters against Britain, the United States, the Soviet Union, and their supporters

MORE BOOKS TO READ

Davies, Kath. *Amelia Earhart Flies around the World.* Columbus, Ohio: Silver Burdett Press, 1994.

Howe, Jane M. *Amelia Earhart: Young Air Pioneer.* Carmel, Ind.:Patria Press, Inc.,1999.

Larsen, Anita. *Amelia Earhart: Missing, Declared Dead.* Columbus, Ohio: Silver Burdett Press, 1992.

Sabin, Francene. *Amelia Earhart: Adventure in the Sky.* Manwah, N.J.: Troll Communications L.L.C., 1997.

INDEX